NATIONAL SONG

Morag Smith was born in Cornwall on the 24th March 1969. She grew up in Essex and on the Isle of Lewis. She had six children and nine grandchildren. She lived for a number of years as a New Age Traveller with her then young family. She returned to Cornwall and graduated from the University of Falmouth in 2019 with a First Class Degree in Creative Writing. She was a member of the Falmouth Poetry Group, and engaged widely with the poetry community in Cornwall. Morag was also an artist, a Zen Buddhist, and an activist, working notably with Clean Ocean Trust. She died on the 26th July, 2023, having received a terminal cancer diagnosis in March of that year.

Also by Morag Smith

Oceana   (Clean Ocean Sailing, 2023)

Spoil   (Broken Sleep Books, 2021)

CONTENTS

ISBN: 978-1-916938-48-9

Cover designed by Aaron Kent

Edited and Typeset by Aaron Kent

Broken Sleep Books Ltd
PO BOX 102
Llandysul
SA44 9BG

PRAISE for *National Song*

These are fearless poems, forged in life's crucible. They put profound intellectual and emotional scrutiny on themes of identity, both personal and political. Morag Smith's work is rooted in her Cornish identity, yet is in active relation to the wider world, where the poet draws from a well of deep experience. There is much wry wit here, and joy in the world, despite life's struggle. She travels the labyrinth of being, keeping hold of the shining thread of language. Here is a beautifully-observed account of a daughter's first childbirth; here she travels back into the maelstrom of her own girlhood in Scotland; here she writes of being swallowed whole by the whale of domesticity and maternal responsibility. Her poetry possesses an abiding sense of the moral landscape, a landscape she has learned from the ground up. This distinguishes her work both ethically and imaginatively. In she bears witness to her experience of social exclusion. She gathers fragments of an often traumatic past, and makes sense of them. Her poems repair damage, and so lead us to believe that healing is possible. These poems now step to their place in the world. I love their resolute purpose, and the hard-won beauty of their truth.
— Penelope Shuttle

Morag Smith's poems erupt with enthusiasm and indignation and pain. Above all they express an unsentimental love of life and especially of Cornwall, tuning in again and again to a profound ancient music. Sometimes it's as if one of the Beats had landed at Falmouth, but there's also a more subtle vein of free verse that another poet from the Isle of Lewis, Iain Crichton Smith, would have recognised. In her shorter lyrics, Smith has an instinctive sense of just how much she should say. There's no superficial polish here, but a rough-cut and often moving sincerity. The poems glitter like Cornish granite.
— John Greening

Morag Smith wrote as she lived her life with a warrior heart. Her passion and enthusiasm for all things poetry is so deeply missed by all of us at Falmouth Poetry Group who were also privileged to call her friend.
I open my mouth/ releasing a stream/ of dark birds/ into the light.
— Rosie Hadden

Morag Smith can never be contained - warrior, revolutionary, nomad, climate activist - a restless, hugely empathetic poet *releasing a stream / of dark words / into the light*
— Katrina Naomi

I have been waiting for poems like this for a long time. Poems that stretch the imagination's reach, hear it snap then stretch it some more. Political, electric, broken, fierce, bloody, alive. I have a feeling that each time I step away from them they reconvene, change, rearrange. A new millennium invites new ways of writing and thinking and *National Song* responds to this invite with fearless energy. Each poem propels me into a place that's familiar and strange and longed for. I am gutted that these are Morag's last poems. 'KIN KIN KIN', she writes, and I hear her, and I hold her hand, and I say yes, I'm here, I'm listening and suddenly we're connected across the void.

— Alyson Hallett

Nature, love, family and travel all gave Morag Smith life experiences that she was able to turn into words on the page. She knew that wanting everything would bring disappointment, but persisted in wanting it all anyway, fighting against the injustices of the world – be that illness, gender, relationships, exclusion and discrimination, or attitudes to travellers and nomads – noting that 'the revolution blossomed' despite 'the spoils of war'. Whether trapped by expectations, social convention, poverty or terminal illness, Morag had something to say and using a poet's skill along with an unnerving honesty and individual approach to language, said it, in forthright canticles and songs of resistance.

These poems will join the memories and images I have of Morag, in university seminars and lectures, at poetry readings and workshops, having lockdown drinks with her partner and I on our village quay, and the day she shyly turned up at my local pub, confusing the landlord and embarrassing me, with a huge bunch of sunflowers she had picked to say thank you for helping her with her writing. Morag was generous, impetuous, thoughtful and gifted, and bears witness to all of these. It is a marvellous collection.

— Rupert Loydell

National Song

Morag Smith

Broken Sleep Books

For Morag.
Dearly missed.

BENEATH ICTIS
(.... an ancient name for Cornwall)

on the sands of Ictis
a figure stands silhouetted by sunrise
one moment an empty horizon
     the next there were boats
a thousand years ago you came
back then I was warrior   woman
you cut the earth   saw my blood flow
to the narrow beach   onto the stones
clots of my life shiny as anemones
     *

now I'm exhausted   so   many   lifetimes
beaten till my teeth rattle like a bag of broken cups
the only path out leads to the sun
and I am without language or gravity
was dragged from the woods
its paths catching like brambles

once I knew about light
now man's prism   wrings colour over the earth

I look for the sun beneath the sun
slip out of my shoes   grip mother earth
feel a drumbeat
maybe it's a heart   a fist
it comes from the core
part sound   part vibration

I connect to a lineage of women
giving birth to each other
Back in the line a warrior
fights for her land and her name
She is me   and I have forgotten
how to be alive inside the earth

I still hear her heart beat
but have lost my way back
to the path beneath the path

HIGHLAND CLEARANCE

you say it's inelegant to sit like that
manspreading all over the velvet that isn't velvet
The sofa matches the armchair
matches the bits of your eyes that are hidden
Between breaths I'm humming the national song
I never learnt
in the imaginary school I never went to
during maths and geography
where I learned the ungreatness of britain

I met a man who ripped off his parent's post office
and left the village he'd always lived in
walking away across the heather
highland roads weren't laid for men
When *I* saw them   I thought of grey treacle
spilling from the back of a truck
saw grass reclaiming and stiff dry rabbit corpses
fur still soft   dotting the hard surface
wanted to stroke them
but instinct cried out against falling in love with the dead

The air in the highlands is thin   breathing territorial
if I belong anywhere it's in the lee of a mountain I've never seen
The heather makes me cry
in england I plucked the small white blooms
wrapped their stalks in foil
walking up and down the promenade like a prostitute
my basket full of luck that didn't work

there were so many gypsies out that day
with shinier luck than mine
I'd travelled to yorkshire   closer to scotland
found the sea rough and opaque   made me homesick

made me remember a moment poised high on the rocks
pink flowers in impossible cracks   wind biting my cheeks
looking down through water deep and clear as sky
menstrual blood spotting the lichen between my cut-down wellies
I tore a strip from the hem of my dress to stop the flow
red lines the length of my leg   drying in the wind

I want to learn a national song that's relevant to me
forgetting the words   even the tune   of freedom songs
sung by my dad on journeys in our precarious family car
chrysalis car   full of tents and cats
my brother and I puking into plastic bags all the way to scotland

In scotland my dad went crazy
pain in his arm from a wound on the battlefield
as we drive past culloden
campbell blood finally spilling into the heather
An untold past   where we were the winners
and everything was lost
Were thistles really sown to stop the barefoot highlanders
as they rushed into battle?
Strands of small stories weave together making a map
a lost history
I learnt gaelic again in a small bedroom in essex

my teacher was dutch   he touched my leg
I thought it an accident
he looked like max headroom   especially in sunglasses
I add him to a list of men wordlessly swapping stuff for sex
bury the list beneath my mind and stop learning gaelic

I wanted to learn my national song
but wasn't anywhere for long enough
My pale ugly skin is actually blue
I'm halved and quartered
post-colonial heritage   reluctance to worship thistles
instead I yearn for the names of herbs
The rocks are alive but everyone acts like they're dead
don't hear them
I press my ear to the sun-warm surface   listen
is this my national song?   my birth right?
trapped as briefly as the cooling heat in the heart of the stone?

BEGINS

it begins in the past in the lee of a field
child hiding
holding a bit of fear
Tells herself
  begin with silence
  begin with hiding things

honking of geese
flying overhead
his hand creeping
inappropriately
their formation
military

OCCUPATION

I see you're a colonialist
what I thought was kindness
was condescension
dismissing the qualities that fail me
you propagate my strengths like a good slave
feed me treats like a dog
forgetting I'm nomadic by nature

IN THE SKULL OF A WHALE

I lived for a year in the skull of a whale
fiddling with my fingernails
forgetting to breathe
touching bone constantly
used the eye holes like windows
becoming the mind of the whale
becoming seventeen times faster
at things I can't remember
and slower
much slower
I was pressed from all sides
couldn't turn
it was easy enough
laying things in narrow lines
but most of the time it felt like a battle
cutting potatoes and carving uneven stars
printing with poster paint
on long rolls of wallpaper
jealous of everyone
My bone cage held me
I expected nothing
small bikes rusted in the yard
and me immobile
watching from my bone window

FRACTURE

lesson 1
friends are enemies
hiding inside friends
holding your secrets like guns
the barrels dark
the bullets dark

the warp and woof
of friendship
is a carpet of secrets
woven on a frame of trust
we held between us like a loom

friendship spills
I have upset you
you are angry with me
I cannot see you
you breathe out freezing fog
ice crystals form on lashes
like a Christmas card
the eyes won't weep for fear
they'll stick
friendship spills into earth
a hot flood melting how it was before
I stand in the mess that melting's left
mourn the snap of strings
the warp
the weft

the tension that had made them sing
surrounds me
in a devastating chorus
that breaks with a noise like gunshot
dark bullets lodge in my gut
I hold them
a homicidal mother
hating the children she made
hugging the pain

lesson 2
I unfriend you
I am a knife
I am broken
I break open
spilling myself wantonly
pouring out of myself in an amniotic flood
that burns as it births
and births in the middle of burning boats
and bridges

we live in different worlds
we acquire air differently
my vision becomes part of my journey

ENEMY FACTORY

The journey reaches pivot point   a crisis moment
I've underestimated
didn't realise how manifold the spanners
launched at the female narrative
how wholeheartedly it was colonized
Almost every country in post-colonial trauma coma
stuck in the recovery room   unaware the operation's over
Is love a bunch of flowers left on the bedside table?

A kitchen   full of steam and smells
the women are cooking   they work and teach
avoiding bombs and bayonets
Behind my rib-coop is the heart of a predator
hunting and gathering precise translations of love
I can't digest the fields and fences of agronomy
its grains go against me
One man glancing askance at his neighbour's land
jealousy flooding his neocortex
firing adrenaline along the blood paths
 Because of this
boundaries necessitate defence   divide people
each yearning for more   plotting for acquisition
demonstrating love by procurement

We want everything   it's never enough
scrabble around making *them* the enemy
fighting over scraps   sending kids to battle
Love isn't leaders intent on gain

safeguarding assets   silently manipulating
seeking to split us apart   nation by nation
skin against skin   gay against queer
trans against feminist
man against feminine   mother   daughter
women and men caught in a monumental battle
clubs and sieves   fists and frying pans
we fight for freedom and space
forgetting we are part of each other

Love isn't a war   won by crushing people
like hunks of dry mud exploding under the heel of our hand
pressure   pain   all turning to dust in a moment
We hail our modernity   ignoring the terror of others
mentally judge them   viewpoint problematically skewed
rejecting or loving   pushing and pulling
head in a bag   for years we peer through the weave
it filters reality into a chess board of colour
Is love for familiar faces the same as
falling in love with your kidnapper?

Gain and Take simmer at the dying edge   Our planet burns
and we demolish embers   collecting ash ceremoniously
air full of dust and smoke   struggling to breathe
like we forgot how to be alive   our minds enmeshed in
formalities
We observe the rules of Gain and Take
our power looks like us but feels like capitalism
it flows to the burning core   Love doesn't conform

refusing to budge she finds reciprocal notes
harmonizing with the whole   reminding us how to breathe
forget enemies
Fearless she dives to the root yammering like a sea bird
KIN KIN KIN

ANXIOUS

caught in the bone cage
startled birds
beat fast wings
against my fragile lungs
breathing is strange
air is hard to take
it hums

the tongue
pushes against a fish-bone pallet
the face hums
the body becomes transparent
impossible to hide inside
the rib rack holds too many birds
crushing them slowly to stillness
wings lock into each other
beady eyes strain sideways
unable to focus
feathered frames hold hearts
that echo through their hollow bones
my chest conceals them
and their panic grows
can't sing
can't fly
eyes pressed into each other's eyes

I open my mouth
releasing a stream

of dark birds
into the light

WILD EDGE

this is the last time
walking the earth together
treading a worn out route
the well worn path
my skin thinner than silk

Blocking the sun with my hand
I see bones like sticks
in a glowing red balloon
grow bigger than my body
I expand beyond boundaries
language a colloquial mashup up
from a dozen locations
you laugh when I try to explain

The last time I said it's the last time
we explored the wild edges of the path
marvelling at the bees
I've a thing for mountains but
the dandelion's
juicy stalk fulfilled me
delivering me from the dark I'd made
   imagining monsters beyond the periphery
   a dangerous wilderness
   entrapment

Seduced by the way my feet fitted the path
I'd carried on through middle age

and now on the brink of old
discover how to be free
Still patterns emerge
becoming a world around me

If I say your name can I stride into the wild?
Will a wolf   its head as high as my chest
stinking
crush my shin in its jaws?
we imagine our world eating us up
slowly as we watch in horror
How have I managed to voyage
from the blood of birth
to this deep ravine and gushing river
full of fast current and gussied at the edges
it rushes on
and I am unable to leave
never thinking this chaos controllable

                              *

When I was eight
I went to cubs with Tim
my friend
on a sleepover
At last gaining entry
this boy's club I couldn't join
frustrated by brownies
I imagined it must be better

For an hour and a half I sat on a chair
excluded from play

inside me the molten rock of resentment
started to move into consciousness
I'd been packed up wrong
didn't belong to perfume and hairspray
A reluctant peacock flouncing
my rosette of boy feathers

Within   the scrawny child quakes
while outside she struts about like a fool
Why would I lie?
abuse is hard enough
without wilfully changing a narrative
already subjective and narrow

I'm prone to exaggerate
but folded this up seven times
and tried to eat it
cracking my teeth
kept it down for years
carefully keeping to the path
patterns printed themselves
on top of each other
this place where I bash my toe
that place where the wolf comes
eating me alive again

TIGER WOMAN

it was dark giving birth in the belly of the whale
    no moon   no stars
just so many ribs and their ivory glow

All night the spirit tiger
prowls   strange in a flesh and water world
raises her heavy paws
steps across the father
asleep in the flood of the floor

you looked at me with dangerous eyes
through an armour of lashes you wore till the end
a small savage creature
holding your pulsing pushing egg
in pale thin arms
strapped and trapped
desperate to reach the mouth of the whale
push through the silver baleen
swim out and up
into the sparkling night

REVOLUTION

the revolution blossomed
a white poppy pushing up from under the skin
demanding peace
protection of innocents
it swam suddenly into our blood
expressing itself like a new hormone
vision uncluttered by thoughts
we stopped   like silence

spoils of war are mothers   daughters
they look at scorched earth between feet that need to run

oh mother   why have you forsaken me

for centuries our clothes smouldered
        when we came too close together
we burst into flames
rolling out of our charred costumes
a great fireball
left them standing
brief empty silhouettes of ourselves
that blew away in the wind

after the revolution bloomed white poppies
on our skin   in our eyes
we lived inside our body   knew it belonged to us
put on our own glittering chastity belts
waiting for him to beg

our terms were systemic absolute and fair
we looked at the scorched earth between our feet
and found ourselves kneeling on grass

we were all on strike
the number of men on our picket lines slowly swelled
he became desperate to resolve things
we dressed our mother in exquisite finery
our faith restored
we washed her till she gleamed
fed hungry children
buried the dead
one day we walked away from our chastity belts
into a new world we had made

HOW TO BEGIN AGAIN

begin by
looking   Untie knots

hope for
clarity   In the beginning

ethereal pleading
unbuckles   in-fra-struc-ture

presents the case
for what-we-are-really

inflight pass grandmothers
aware I didn't see you

with the eyes first
Feet groping the same edges

balance your levelheadedness against insanity
in the kitchen

begin here   cooking up a cake/storm
red dress dusted in memories

SEA WOMEN

my body stands like that
more liquid than a man's
I claim the mineral rights inherent in
my supplicating palms   this body mine
but mined and mined and never mine
the copper in the knee that pins the wind
iron smelted to steel within my mind
and I have cavities inside where I
have always been afraid
man spins his wool of words   he clothes us
now we swim   naked in the white wash
striking out   for somewhere new
where we have never been
and never been and never been

MEDICINE

earth-body alchemist
finger and thumb
pinching the shaft of an owl's feather
dancing the sea-spiral
dressed in darkness
dense as the derelict mines
under our hills

weaving energy
into that vital stone
arms   scything serpents
legs beat the mud drum
follow the sand song
I sing through my bones

you who turn oil into flight
fear my prayer
hear it coming like weather
warm front
storm dark
a spinning canticle
pulling it
all to ground

ACKNOWLEDGEMENTS

Many thanks to the editors of the following anthologies in which some of these poems first appeared: *Moroven, Oceana* (Clean Ocean Sailing), *24 Voices for Change* (Poetry Point), *26 Places in Cornwall/26 Tyller yn Kernow*.

LAY OUT YOUR UNREST

Printed in the USA
CPSIA information can be obtained
at www.ICGtesting.com
LVHW041352040924
789919LV00007B/129